yesterday's dawns

avi sato

springwaterspress

Print ISBN 978-0-9877194-4-7
Digital ISBN 978-0-9877194-5-4

Issued simultaneously in print and electronic formats.

Published in Canada.

for my parents

who always believed

even when i did not

absolving

driven beyond the madness
of culture's expectations
you plunge your head
beneath streams' surfaces
drinking liberating breaths
of hatreds' liquid memories
only to quench minds'
thirsts for longing
with the thoughtful celibacy
of silenced revolution

where rainfall has begun
your head shimmers
with stars' unyielding distanced presence
no longer dependent
on your imagined earth's position
in a galaxy of echoed constructed realities
of soft feminines and penetrated impermanence
facing dominances' proposals of privilege

you once cast nets
on waves of unnavigable desires
and flung lusts' hopeful suitors
lifelines of bone-shattering submission
escaping with no life left worth the name
yet beyond pasts' discomforting rhythms
you rise burned from the unseen corpse
of gazes fueled by inflamed predictive gaze

you touch a self
first reborn of undesirability
shaped to forms unknowable
amid hazy beliefs of roles
best left to unlearned animals
seeking procreative supplication
between pleasured sanctuaries
of scriptural misinterpretation
and often viewed otherings
of your unabsolving completeness

you see the river
of passed sorrows

of pretended conformity

that sacrifices its sparkled beauties

with a depth of surface tensions

stripped from your tomorrows

to wake alone

embodying dialogs' lengthy desires

amid fields of horizontally dissatisfied norms

longing

standing by the stream
you contemplate walking into the water
yet its glistening waves
belie the consuming terrors
of bitter memories
that await your touch
below the reflective surface

shadows between ripples
cry in anticipation of your feet
while the conformity of daily life
presses you forward
to drink its depths
into lungs moments from an end embraced

breathing its liquid dreams
into futures absent of all but echoes
nearly forgotten
gives hope where none lived
in the hours of your mind

yet those tomorrows paint soundscapes
of overwhelming noise
and place hands on your back
that propel body
to shallow moistened graves
that call from underworlds
unbelieved until this moment

this shall not be the mistake
of which they speak
but sanctuary amid others
whose voices tear your peace
from itself
and shatter calm waves
with movements unpredicted yet observed

beauty no longer lives
in the living
yet in barely glimpsed days
of missing remembrances

simplicity returns in your image

without new times of loss

lesson

a simplicity overwhelms
with its pervasive desires
in your eyes' ubiquitous reflections
yet depth oppresses
and relents not a moment
from words of momentary pleasure
and thoughts of tomorrows'
unending games

you wake
with the sensation of incompleteness
before hours of targeted self-assassination
amid linguistic exhortations
of introspective love
and outward performances

no homes are obvious
to save you from the dreams
you left behind
to open your eyes

into the stereotype
you now understand
as ordinary daily life
long paths from the precise meanderings
of living rivers

your footsteps stumble
with each brush of the earth
as you take no more time
to decide
while confronted by a gaze
less benign than unknowing
yet pretending to great wisdoms
of ages not yet come

stars

daylights' devolve toward fragrances
shimmering above streams
unconscious with the magical assumptions
that dance midair
at the moment of dusk
to taste into your soul
seconds of harmonies
yet silenced
upon your seeking lips

no darknesses
consume that willingness
behind your eyes
to escape from todays' thoughts
somehow all-consuming
yet unwanted
in their sensory pervasiveness
and levitate within yourself
into skies slightly tinged
with a blue

lost to all
but the most imaginary of eyes
before the wink
of the new moon's startled face

polyphonies of reason
decry rational answers
from galleries unknowable and unbelieving
yet you step through mountain horizons
into waking images
of footfalls on virgin grasses
watered by immaterial rivers
whose tongues amaze ancient cities
with mythologies of uncreation

your smile confronts
deaths' myriad provocations
with unrealized lyrics
amid dreamless eternities
of cycles remaining unfulfilled
in their emptinesses
while blacknesses' false nirvanas

present concentric rings of entrapment

toward fingers

not yet able to touch your depths

you awake to skies afire

from idiosyncrasies

with eyes straining to perceive

in the absence of proximate stars

while unending twilights

creep into mornings

yet a mirror within you

teaches joy in unknowing

previous

you lie awake
consumed by impermanence
that has soaked
within your very being
yet troubles
with the sensations of fire
that only derive from a world
beyond your dreams'
collapsed horizons

no sanctuary is built
in your imagination
to hide you from the light
that dispels shadows
that you have built for yourself
where you take refuge
from troubling visions
plaguing your memories

unlearning your past

overwhelms with stimulus
a body no longer alive
to the touch of friends' fingertips
beckoning you out of mountain streams
where you submerge desires of rebirth
in their frigid shallows

rebirth no longer intrigues you
in contrasts' stark visions of tomorrow
while similarity obsesses verses
once believed lost
into footsteps
shaken from calm rivers' pathways
toward bridges
not once safe in their crossings

tomorrow hovers wild
at the edge of a longing
where divergent words
enfold realities' failures
but call you into
twilights of inaction

in this moment you yet stumble

through single imprints

of soul on sand

trapped by currents that cannot reach you

yet which you decide to embody

since once in a time

you seek not to relive

but forget exists

only within your

creative distress

idolatry

in the light of morning
the gentle current of your voice
speaks into the corners
still consumed by the darkness
of twilights unending
but with faltering steps
the shimmering of reflections
blinds me to its depth

i step across streams
yet lose myself in their relentless drive
toward salt's stark bitterness
yet the taste comforts me
as i breathe your unspoken touch
across my hands
and strip daydreams' expected metaphors
for their liquid centers

before the altar of burned idols
i pray

yet the flames of your mind
have not yet released
the fear of yesterday's sun's
planned obsolescence

but my eyes do not shy
from the shimmering fires within you
and with your light
a cascade of welcome cataracts
sweeps beyond my hastily constructed
fences of doubt
to nourish a core
once thought by all lost
by its own magnetism
yet you call me to wild sanctuaries
within your spirit

careless

glass stained with memories of your touch
contrives to cast shadowed light
behind the prismed walls of unconscious terror
tasted by forgotten lips in concrete pasts

unread books stack toward promised sunlights
yet supporting pages cast no enlightened smiles
toward tomorrows' expectations of another you
lost in a history of appropriations

reflected in closed eyes
your passion burns
with the presence of an extinguished flame
awaiting new kindling to be resurrected
in the image of forgiveness yet buried

secret within voices' histories
sung without harmonies
in their presuming solitude
to walk toward shivering leaves

seeking any pain but that of your presence
with its warm embrace
and shocking beauty

you call into darknesses
never without their lightnings' flashes
while echoes return to your mouth
bypassing senses' quivered
to recreate pleasures' performances
within scents of dawns' ubiquitous streams

yet fears' astonished lyrics shimmer rainbows
above calm ponds
tearing untruths from possibilities
and plunging the unthinkable
into next moments' absolutes

you offer no sanctuary
but in you
and that price i would pay willingly
if only it were not a self no longer in flight
from empathic longings

within your caring arms

enfolded around a body

i seek yet lose

to press into your care

awakeness

no essence of yesterday
constrains the ideas
that float through memories
mingling with truth
yet consuming
with their ever-present demands
for present realities
overlayed with the image of things feared
yet impossible to ignore in their obsession

unwelcome terrors
dance their footsteps on concentric paths
within a mind overwhelmed
by the grief for lives no longer present
and pasts lost into a darkness
that never gave them the chance
to be consummated into tomorrows' rebirth

pages of senses' touched dreams of self-control
sink beneath molten stones

driving them toward earths' theoried centers
yet lacking in the presence
once believed within those thoughts
to define the object of the only action
still to be important
to forgotten pictures of happiness

calm truths pass ungrasped
in their simplicity
above the segregated banks of rivers unstoppable
of emotion liquified by imagination
into footpaths of moistened sand
with each broken pebble
a single blade's stroke away
from its perfect silence
yet never finding its partner
within overwhelmed mazes of absence

gaze

dawn's beauty
collapses the shadows
of unremembered twilights
with its crystalline vision

unknowable fates
dance along
the edge of civilization
atop holy mountains
imprinted on tablets
rote and written

morning grasses
shimmer into existence
not possible in the present
of moments before
when they hid their faces
from your eyes

a wren's calming melodies

caress winds
toward adding their plainsong
to daybreak's echoes
of reincarnations long forgotten

reflections' counterpoint
frolics unhurriedly into being
as if it had never paused
for rest
before the moon's obsequious face
hidden by mists' modesties

edges of movement
catch visions barely capable
of discerning their existence
yet certain that a presence
denies the loneliness
of forced exclusion

a subtle belonging
overwhelms the spirit
with its undeniable wish

for an inclusion

that is not of touch

and spoken greeting

but an animal intensity

that is tasted in the air

yet soothing in its distant proximities

forever lands on skin

with the forgiveness

of the slightly out of reach

and the comfort of speaking lyrics

into the songs of the soul

that only sound into the absence

and shiver within strings

of harmonics unprepared

kami

beauty shivers
slightly beyond the doorpost
into unreality
from this darkened room
of negative development
basking in the red-pigmented light
of predawn shadows' ubiquity

a cascade of rainbows
breaks
the visual silence
of traumatic self-reflection
yet it shakes you
not from the half-slumber of remembrance
into the daylight
beyond your unenlightened night

as you step from entombed cloisters
into the brilliance of morning's presence
a sensation overtakes

a desire for becoming
with the knowledge of life
surpassing yesterday's rocky
walls of separation

with the unforeseen touch
of petal to face
you step beyond a time of thought
into one where the newness of emotion
not of goodness or evil
but breathing a fluid essence of life
rebuilds history in its image

you taste the vision of birdsong
perfuming winds unseen
yet brushing against nascent hairs
striving toward sunshine
on arms no longer covered
in their shame
but raised in adoration
of panic's absence

walking paths of moistened streamside stones

rebirths your soul from past lives

into the openness of a morning

literal in its becoming

yet possessing the depth of an awakening you

in oneness with the gods

within the world

faithless

divergent raindrops darken glass' vibrant echoes
while sunlight dances on spherical surfaces
and becomes trapped
behind your eyes' expectant wonder

unbecoming shapes transform
within your memory
to days once thought forgotten
yet somehow relived in your imagination
reborn into times never once extant

the paper of sheets rings crisp
against the darkness of midday
closeted through vast retellings
of viciously inaudible prayers to forget
yet spring from past logic
into nighttime's lack of awe

straightened beliefs
clash against half-forgotten bodies

askew in their obviated negatives

and insipid silenced protests

become screams

not of delight

but curiously proximate to willing ears

you are the voice of dread

become doubt

faced with collisions of sympathy and spectacle

striking down sensations of projected myth

and hallucinations' hopes

in the image of their

burdens of untruth

pasts

small hours' subjective proximity
clouds a vision of limitless lakes
beyond horizons dominated by human
        intervention
and becomes it toward imaginations
of fateless forests thoroughly desired

echoing starlight reveals little
of hedgerows' overwhelming sameness
against backdrops of once-present mothers
natural in their conceptionless presence
yet consumed
by their millennia of disbelief

torn from their roots
trees of pleasant abandon
hide behind veils or willing mists
among pathways of pasts
stretching behind memories institutional and
        vague

to hallucinations' hopeful unrememberings
of profligate greens
and lush lonelinesses

unseeing visions taste truths
unprofound and proximate
within slivered moonbeams
shocking in their undistanced simplicities
yet unthinkable in their recreation
as echoed northern facets present
against contemporary failures of foresight

fresh rains' scents abandon
a land of brightened canopies' absence
into pastured sameness
yet pausing a breath's bitter moment
to shimmer into existence
pretemporal idealizations of self-denials
unfulfilled in their delights of eastern harmonies
become dissident

if you

to you

who once stood at my side

i can do nothing

but remember you in your absence

as you who touched

the depths of my soul

with unending fires of provocation

to shift myself

into a light

that once i thought

would blind me

but standing protected by you

i face it

as one built to stand

atop ships' masts

not within their bowels

sheltered from storms

a vision of you

haunts not my dreams
but my waking moments
between rest
with the touch of effortless history
dragged into the present
by the motion that simply cannot end
and a being that echoes beside my soul
that is not simply within me
but within all i see
and each leaf i taste
in its visual aura

within your spirit
conducted into being by a limitless presence
you drive me to be a different self
than i would embody without you
and toward futures
unthinkable in my passionate loneliness
and cultivated segregation

yet i am more myself in you
than ever i could have been alone

and less a part of normalcy
than i once thought i would have to be
just to survive

you are not the hat floating on the winds
but those wind spirits themselves
that raise up the ideas
that inhabit the space behind my eyes
and speak through my lips
with a vision that you embodied
not as yourself but as me within your heart

while you spoke to me
through your own tongue's whispered cadence
directly toward words
landing on my skin
with a breath
i may never forgive myself for having lost
yet savor in its remaining beauty

sisters

slip gently behind lines
held by those not quite awake
enough to be enemies
yet somehow distant in their distress
at your existence

taste their thoughts on the air
as you walk before eyes cast upward
in an attitude of loss
while they become
the very image of distrust

breathe through the winds of their desires
calmed only by the brutality within them
unable to win against the terror of persecution
in the depths of depravities' unadmitted lusts
at your otherness

stand peacefully overlayed against horizons
now silhouetted before a sunshine

they pray to for deliverance
out of foreign lands become their own
from where escape is their only refuge

yet they realize nothing
examining your skin as if it were unknowable
in its enveloping presence
while theirs covers sins of judgment
and grasps glass-housed stones of hatred

begin within their visions
and inhabit their forgotten dreams
if you must
as in their hatred
you become the obsession
of their unimaginable night terrors
visited not on your head but elsewhere
in their insatiable capacities
to denude your lips' lyrics of self-compromise

end not within their minds
but fulfill daydreams' enviable silences

from behind staged curtains of modest
        reawakenings
taken from your bedside
but returned
carried on the winds of tomorrow's dawn
        hesitations

awakened self-directed photographs stir
reflected into your thoughts
from dark words spoken into ears
deaf with their ubiquity
and face not them
but one your fingers grasped as new family

beyond

winds of desire do not conquer you
yet standing before their unveiled gaze
you drink their displeasure
and walking from their thrones
into wild places unmapped
you are overwhelmed
by their unrequited absence of love

no sands are carried on the breeze
as you awake
into the darkness of the sacred mountains
yet you feel the light from within yourself
at the newfound freedom
that sees no limitations
imposed from outside
on your self-fulfilled dawns

a sparrow touches feet to branch
above your head
striking the eyes

not with loneliness but its inverse
as its melody carries
into the dew-soaked undergrowth
and finds no critics to answer
among its kind
and you taste the first day of freedom

noon sun enlivens hopes of solitude
rebuilding pasts
in the image of a new interpretation
as you donate your naked body
to the secrecy of the lake
where in newness the chance of movement
without the presence of eyes
astounds in ways
you know it should not

you compose fresh autobiographies
in styles before left untouched
in their simplicity
and speak to the animals
gathered not in the judgment you left behind you

but the beauty of interest
in a human that others lost
in assumptions of evolutionary superiority

breathing out images of unobjectified peace
you sink beneath sunset's last glimpse
over distant peaks before firelight
and begin anew
in the knowledge that
in this place
you once more have found yourself safe
and sleep

perhaps

trap blatant snowflakes

at the edge of unwieldy tongue tips

before they may alight

on darkened pathways

beneath footsteps uncertain

gaze beyond clouded hills

to breathe sunrise

into the glimmer of reflection

showing beneath

from the distant city's

polluted obsessions

walk unsteadily

beside troubled stream beds

long become concrete

while your feet sense the bones of unsainted

       martys

become unwelcome reminders

of reincarnations unrequited

love outside coloring books' delineated
              unsubtleties
while unnoticed tremors
gather beneath skin
to plot new campaigns
of civilized rebellion from within
to plunge eyes' hopes
into new heights of unknown beauties
dreamed of but thought lost
into a world whose lusts describe passions'
              elaborate rules

but escape callings
where you taste into rebellions their lifeblood
echoed from afar
yet mere arm-lengths away
above sheets of silk
rough with their unworn dignity

placid in piety's unpopular imaginations
while into still airs of ices' abandonment

you stifle laughter
from companions' unsuitable to ears' of friendship
absent before it posits truth
into your life

popularity contests overwhelm horizontal
              expectations
and drill liquid memories
into regrets' performative unimpassioned
              memories
shivered onto diary pages
best left to flame
yet cherished in their acceptances
guaranteed toward adulthoods of guilt

a simple touch
saves you from futures unthinkable yet ubiquitous
while hearts' rhythmic entanglement
presupposes branches of missing olives
grasped as you do limbs
to bridge rivers no longer absent
their beauties ebbed within in your image

hands

seek within the secret collapse of worlds
made numerous in the image
of your often dreaming mind
before the sunset of a day already forgotten

look inside yourself
for those things that you have lost
as they have been stolen
behind a back unturned
while you watched a culture of thieves
ply their trade with your permission

no longer cry archetypes of tearful melodies
into darkness
while performed martyrdoms
plague your compatriots
into karmic balance sheets
misinterpreted in their inegalitarian blindness

speak truth not to power

but to minds
raped in the shadows
of yesterday's freshly-absolved guilts
before confessionals
whose births replaced the shrines
lost to progress

embrace not absence
but the embodiments of ways
lost in their suffering
through expectation
of life's merited goallessness

believe into action a presence
between opposing sides of unspent coins
grasped by clutching fingers
whose owners seize control from selves
unwilling to sit shiva for the beauty
they know not they've lost

pretend acceptance
to emotion-scarred faces of solitary penetration

to find upright lotuses
amid cushions of willing stones
caressed by streams of unconscious experience

breathe the uncertainty of living freedom
into the presumed hopelessness
of unfaithful lip-servants' pursuits
of pretended converted zeal
amid lightly-veiled immodesties
of hatreds' vocal fists

kneel at dawn's becoming whispers
tasting mornings into your soul
as you touch new sisters' hands
in welcome

smile

upon rounded stones
cast down by winds
of pasts' unremarkable waters
you show the face
my memory draws
onto surfaces slick
with night's blossoms' reflections

fallen leaves break
into mind's creation
amid lapping waves
to turn your voice's clarity
in my recently banished dreams
to mere echoes
of a civilization
born in you

unbelievable lyrics
transform
the river's endless susurration

from nature

to human stories of wisdom unrealized

and enlightenment lost

in a moment of unclarity

yet you reached

out of that almost-brightness

to place hands on hands

and lips where lips seek

to find their partners

to free me

from obsessions' lustful demonstrations

of their instantaneous power

drawing me

from the reality of my now

to create peace

following you up a mountain

not of your making

but discovered in each second

as something indistinct

from the you

that i breathed in love
and a confusion
of unnamed sensations

between trees
you press plucked flowers
between my fingers
and draw me toward the ground
in shouts of ecstatic gratefulness
for the smell of life
and reward me for my smiles
with those of your own

clearing

forests abandon me
into their unloving arms
as i contemplate the gratitude
i should feel
walking amid falling leaves
but somehow yet again
am missing

sunlight falls through branches
onto my face
and i am confused by it
for a moment
then longer
as i strain to sense
whether it is hot
or simply a new sense
of having not breathed enough lately

the crack of a branch
behind me

in this instant
breaks the stillness that wasn't there
except in my mind
as i walked through the noises

having jumped as electrocuted from sleep
my racing heart struggles
to return
to the pleasant meditation of footsteps on a path
that is instantaneously more than metaphor

the misunderstanding of pattern
distills itself in me
in the question of which foot takes the first
                movement
to right or left
and in that decision
i am paralyzed by unrequited fear

if butterfly wings stimulate hurricanes abroad
in what disaster will any motion create
in a life precarious at its best

and this being an ungrateful self
in a paradise of undergrowth

a maple leaf falling
not quite on my forehead
but brushing my left eye
as it is carried on a sudden gust
wakes me from inaction
and i give up the thought of choice
to run

dashing
headlong between cloying roots
destined to fall
but giving exactly no fucks
in a race with mind
to outrun the fears
like chutes
of fresh hope
to strangle my cries for escape

i brush between unidentified limbs of a lifeform

in green

to a clearing

where no great view opens

but the impact of absence surrounding me

tells me in no uncertain terms

this is no dream

and thinking won't save me

breathe now

as next time

it will be too late

to run

lost

you speak of loss as teacher
yet in me it tastes of emptiness' abandonment
       reality
shattered into mirrored fragments
that never melt in the mouth
in years and lifetimes

i wake mornings to drenched pillows
and entire percussion solos
fracturing my chest
from the panic of feeling your arms holding me
and encountering in this awoken moment
the opposite of fusion within me

absence changes
giving me no opportunity to learn
adapt
tolerate
in the instant
that taste as unfriend

but familiar

today it is another moment of you
that speaks inside my mind
a memory
not quite real
but created
in a voice of you
somewhere beyond daydream
but unlike fiction

life is different since you were here
with spoken words silenced
and fluid genders
held up to a light
they hid from

a world of opposites would greet your
             reincarnated soul
polarizing in their extremities
that would shock your closed eyes
into fearing openness

expressions of joyful abandon
live with hateful neighbors
as punches replace harsh words
and perceptions expel once-accepted cultures
and bleach all futures white

would you hide
from today
and seek
new paths
of escape
as i do
or take shaken fingertips against your palm and
            stand

i have no doubt
yet loss teaches me nothing
while i shiver behind terrorized barricades
and silence angry words
from those who once ignored
and even tolerated

you once taught me life in the beauty of a single
      birdsong
and love in the touch of a leaf

where is that lesson
amid this fire

prayer

kneel blinded by eyes unwilling to be present
before the makeshift altar
offering nothing but my unworthy self
knowing i alone am the goddess to whom i speak
      and whose praises i sing
an archetype created in my own image of hopeful
      transaction
i will live fueled by your love

i push away desires for death in return for your
      strength
but that love resides within me
and in its absence i become more aware that i may
      seek nowhere else for it
and when it comes not there is no hope
no dream of pleasure that comes with its own
      segregate truth
no oneness separate from myself to be discovered
where that strength resides between the tips of
      my interlaced fingers

and comes not
i know now that it is impossible
i am destined to worship the self-goddess in
        circles of eight and a hundred
endlessly

but remain broken from love
torn from strength
as the love of others flows from my lips
and caresses the untasted future from my
        fingertips
and the strength i incite in you echoes on the
        pathway
floating within the stream on tomorrow's
        enlightenment
but is silent within me
as i breathe desperation
into today's bright sunlight
felt as shade

apart

you wish not to be beautiful
but to disappear
beneath the ubiquitous gaze
of expectations
judging books not by covers
but distanced desires
of momentary passion

to escape
from the watchful meanderings
of eyes intoxicated by feminine presence
outside the walls of museums' signs
crying look but not touch

yet it is the looking
that consumes your every breath
and builds a home
wherein you cry unseen
seeking simply to walk
over its threshold

toward forests of sanctuary
to be hidden between trunks
of unspoken comprehension
under canopies of opacity

no words fall willingly on ears
beyond stimulus' saturations
and touch imparts electrical passions
making thoughts of solitude
sweeter in their impossibilities

to walk paths
where others no longer speak into silence
or feel the need to interact
with lips
or tongues
or fingertips
but drifting
as island of self

you cry in desperation
yet others disappoint

in their presence

not still in unwelcome noise
and oppressive proximity
they hurt with their willingness to follow
paths to inclusion
where you seek the misunderstood joys
of living beyond the walls
of humanity

bedtimes

from the darkness before dawn
i look across the river
and see nothing
but artificial stars
on the opposite bank
reminding me of the shame
of yesterday

friends' words of forgiveness
ring something more than hollow
as they echo
with a laughter of artifice
i am no longer sure
was only in my mind

i hesitate
to name what karmic unraveling
has woken me
from a restless night
lest i breathe

more life into it
than already lives in its depths
as its fingers grip my neck
more tightly
and i struggle
paralyzed against cotton sheets
pressing gently above my face

their unforgettable expressions
torture me
against the back of my eyes
as i open them
to the near blackness
of cityscape
reflected on my window
parsed through linen mesh

jeans brush against skin
as i recklessly clothe myself
without turning on lights
and the enveloping smell
of hoodie and hairspray

mingle to remind me
of a happiness
only hours past its ending
but only performed
for their benefit

campus sleeps
around me
while the oppressed notes
of early songbirds
mingle with trees' wind-induced tones
and my footsteps
tracing heartbeats
against the packed earth
by the river

the forest embraces me
with its unsilence
and vigilance
knowing somehow my sleepless nights
and practiced acting
against the normalcy

of other visitors

perhaps from the timing
but palpable fear
resonates against treetrunks
and turns silhouetted leaves
to demon skylines
at the hint of dawn glow

i serve no practical purpose
yet one last moment
of regret
captures me
as i return
to bed
within the river
and await
the cleansing elements
to steal
everything
but my soul
in a light

less solar than spiritual

and a new night

captures me

dawn

i reach out and touch your skin and it calms me
my heart beating as if my chest were in my head
but i am still unsure whether you are lying beside
       me
after a day of loudness
screaming both within me and from your lips
once soft against mine
now tearing cells from their neighbors
with an intensity i thought impossible
as you demanded freedom that i never withheld
and passion i couldn't have predicted

you left in whirlwinds of sound
only missing trumpets from the royal procession
accompanying your footsteps
leading from my door to a new one
that you had found for yourself
without me having noticed
where you had discovered a self without me
and others with you

i cry but in the depths of my eyes
the newfound passion within you
it caressed my soul
in ways i was never able to give you reason to
             smile
so i breathed stillness in time
knowing i was unwelcome in the pattern you
             searched
and finally found

yet that one call
of panic and distress
no longer peaceful in the loss of me
but frantic in what you had never expected
in a shift from my passivity
to those who feel desire
that you said you wished to experience
in its fullness
in its passionate truth
and demanding unity of purpose

but passion is uncontrollable in its nature
and the years of giving in to nothing more than
        kisses
between chaste lips of peaceful subtlety
opened a rift between your expectations
and the demands of one who wanted more than to
        hold
but to enter and possess
to own and dominate
control with the self rather than the mind

and you had forgotten how to say no not simply
        to power
but to presence
another with all the perspectives
of on and in and thru
not simply beside and with
as you realized it was not being trapped
but a freedom within the self
that is born only of confidence
and knowledge that passion does not arise
and domination is outside the box

where you are safely cuddled
and held
for yourself and not for what you may give
or the momentary sensations

yet that ended suddenly
as the blood from yourself
mingled with the death of our past
body and mind become the one that you searched
and in vain you wished to put it back
a life into a happy box of smiled complacency
and redness into a newly torn self

but are you here
i ask myself
and ask you
and you say nothing
yet shiver in the dawn light
among blankets still clean
the image of beautiful calmness
as you smile a new beginning
a permanent peace for us

without the restless search for others

and i return to breathing

as i touch your face

haze

sheets entomb me as i lie
lost in the white that i saw brief moments ago
but now dark
where light went
i know
but feel as a surprise
how long have i been here
lost in tears
where i am possessed by a loneliness
i once thought was a sign of youth
but realize is a missing piece
of me that i had dreamed
would be nothing more than pain

yet it has transformed me
in its chemical penetrations
to a me wrapped in tears
looking at a window
where thru is impossible
in its darkness

and the flickering of the single candle
whose flame has mesmerized me in its novelty
each second dancing in ways i never could
yet always tried to mirror
at least in my head

what have i lost
i ask myself
and realize there is nothing
that i had before
i do not have now
but the feeling of smiles
that were once natural
were lost with the infancy
i left behind long ago
and you taught me to find again
which i have now forgotten

i close my eyes onto the moisture
and it stops
as you are projected onto the back of lids
and dance far more in keeping with the candle

still touching their outsides
but it has been a single day
since you walked into my vision
sat beside me before takeoff
and by landing were inside my head
to populate my dreams
yet only to become a human bird
at next airport and leave
as wind takes tree offsprings
and individuals become streams
lost to themselves

i touch your name with eyes reopened
realizing the truth of possible loss
i had once thought to shield myself from
endlessly
yet with each simulated keypress
i bring the danger of future absence
toward me
and i cannot bring myself to care
i miss you

not sure what i had thought
that you were awake and awaiting
in the darkness of your own bed
distant yet likely a mirror
of this room
impersonal in its transience

but moments' endless travel ends quickly
as vibration meets sound and the candle jumps
just outside my peripheral vision
and its shadows startle me
as hand opens and head twitches
while phone slides from sheet to floor
and i grab for it three times
before i raise it to my face and squint

back next week
come see me
you touched my soul somehow

i drift to sleep
no longer feeling the sheets as tomb

but wings of breath holding me
in pure lands' cotton fingers

i awake to a blank screen of absent power
the long-cold wick burned black
stark in the brilliant sun
streaming across crumpled self-wrappings
and smile in the confusion
of whether dream or reality
gave me peace in the darkness

observation

why do you

dear butterfly

pause for a moment

on my sorrowful self

and treat me

as a tree's time ravaged leaf

not preparing to fall

but still in its subtlety

tasting nutrients

living thoroughly

yet unbroken from the branch

while my tears

do nothing to enrich me

nor to fill my veins

with the breath of motion

while i curl

fetal self

yet no longer within

the moisture of another

seeking solace within

yet finding only the richness
of salt

expressed as a river
broken it's confines
loosed from self-imposed banks
where once i kept locked dreams

as wings disappear from my vision
no echo overwhelms me
their beating gentle
against an air i struggle to breathe
yet somehow i reflect
the tiny shimmering
they embody
as they picked their way
from lashes to fingertips
newly soaked with eyes' outpourings
taking my self-salt
to distant leaves
more attuned to freedom
in their fixedness
than i have felt

for a moment

in leg-bound flexibility

not separate from life

remembered as part of earth

but separate

as sorrow's waters

run deeply to flooding

creating channels between me

and the world of

such winged beauty

hope

truthful ambiguities
collapse into clouds of imagined memory
recreated in the image of hope
once lost and found
disappeared again
in this moment
never to be unearthed

yet qualifying itself
as my history
as others believe its verisimilitude

unquestioning now
but doubting
without a word
the reality within
while letting float into subconsciousness
its artifice

who understands the dreaming ventures

of uncertain minds
where trouble alights
with each door knocked
and word shouted
into the darkness
of midday's shivering

a flickering image
of yesterday's intended pain
gives way to today's
unintentional triggers

believe in a better reaction
to overwhelmed senses
but expect it not of me

as hope disappeared
just as thoroughly
as notions of earth's flatness
in the face of dawn
over unvisited horizons

reborn after their solemn diving
beyond the bay
without touching that hated moisture
of ocean

prediction arrives
with the certitude of the unseeing touch
landing as whip on unveiled flesh
expectation torturing this moment
and the next
until it is disappointed
by my paralysis

speak silence into a darkness
unshaken by movement and solitude
into a stillness unbroken by whispering
and capture me with closed eyes
whose motion quivers slightly
in the moon's imagined halo

essence

touch my soul
with the lips i once imagined
against mine
only to speak darkness
to a light now extinguished
by arctic winds

taste my soul
with the eyes i held
before a gaze
i once believed embodied compassion
and know now
are the ice of the northern earth
collapsed into a pair of shining globes
overshadowing dawn's beauty

swallow my soul
with the arms i longed
to have wrapped around me
not beneath linen

but atop cliffs
before plunging myself from their heights
into the waterfall
awaiting my corpse below
as you walked away
without a moment of glancing

capture in me
the love that once i felt
but now can find no longer
in its reflection

sing in me
a song without notes
onto paper that asks no questions
and tells only lies

believe in me
a vision of a future
alone but not lonely and aflame
with the movement of the stars
in the heavens

to transform myself
into the one
you once touched
and tasted
and swallowed whole
and remade
in the image of your love
for me

give me your hand
and step into the void
as i scream
for time
to wait
just one more second
before stepping you
off my stage

echoes

dear you
who lost yourself
in the mirror
of your own creating

who designed a you
to find again
in futures distant
that you must now create
and feel nothing of joy
in your mornings
but only in the oblivion
of losing yourself
to the liquids and smokes
of the moment

there is no you
in that far place
of your imagination
but only here in now

and in the change you see within

there is a loss
you cannot see
and in you i breathe new life
as you once tasted
within my soul

and gave me tomorrow's spirit
today
when i could hold it
and ride those winds of rainbows
toward unseen stars
and become a me that you believed
shimmered in my eyes
that i couldn't see
or even imagine
but was there
a reflection of you

but in your artificial mirror
the blackness of your reflected imagination

consumes your moment
and turns to fire
the stream of soul
in which you swim
a single droplet on the ocean
unique and distinct

a taste of orange
in a sea of tranquil blue

awake
and put the dreams to bed
and be today
as tomorrow you would wish to remember

as in me you once put your faith
i speak new words
to echo that hope in you

seeing fire within your eyes
and beauty you thought lost forever
in your words

perceptions

i sit and try to create a new perspective
on a past that haunts my dreams
but they return in my waking seconds
to destroy the temple i have built to worship
      happiness

i walk through shadowed valleys of premature
      death
without signs of reincarnation
doubting the truth of existence with each footstep
and straying from myself as i never imagined
      possible

i leave my mind and float above salted rivers
and dry mineral baths that no longer clean bodies
      and rocks
but taste of metal on my tongue
as blood flows from delicate wrists

although i remember no moment

of clear division
of skin
or touch
even of metal
yet instantly i feel myself weaken
as internal moisture meets air
and shivers no longer come and go

they simply are within me
as breathing shallows and twilight appears in
            afternoon sun
with its collapse of the brightness in my eyes
as life drains from them and freedom calls

a silence shatters
the concentration
and i am returned to a reality that i had thought
            finally ending
as i look at dry skin
and realize hallucinations' implied follies

no memory of separation of flesh from flesh

walked through my daydream
as it was nothing more than wishful
        unpleasantness
on a new pathway to desired self-annihilation

not to be outdone in my hopes
an unreality presented itself
and i lost my footing
and drank it not as wine
but water in gasping wholeness
as its salt coursed past my metaled postprocessed
        tongue

there is no silence sitting here
in messy half lotus
wondering where i went wrong
in a life that i never dreamed would last into these
        interminable years
of mindlessness alone

birds chatter

as voices drift from trails distant yet nearly within
         arms' reach
speaking languages i know i understand
in theory
but whose users experience feelings
i only know by name

not by experience
nor depth
nor even shallow adherence
and this saves me
they say
from the sadness and misery and acts of self-
         violence
that transform the joyful and grateful

to shimmering wrecks
overgrown with spiritual weeds
unable to speak simple words of enlightenment
or visit places of calm within their souls amid
         crying and screaming

yet

in my peace

i hear

nothing

but a dream of no tomorrows

consumed by a terror that grips me by wrists

       moistened with hopeful redness

flowing over the grasp's unseen fingers

as they twist

not in wind

but tearing breath from flesh's disgusting future-

    corpse

but memory feels of muscle

like piano chords tickling beneath fingertips of

      long ago practice

teaching me scalar patterns

for unexciting self-examination

which is the only music within me

it echoes

in its rhythmic manifestations of breath

and ends only in repetition
to a point
where i lose track of their overlays
in a canon firing blank verses
through ears pierced
by fragmentary private conversations

overheard through wind's sharing prerogatives'
        ubiquitous disregard for real-world
        cookie warnings
tasting more of dough
than sustenance
yet reverberating between blades of uneven grass

yet those thoughts loosen their grip
as i pry unseen and unknowable sinews
from the consciousness they tear at
and speak aloud
to inform ears
they are not connected to death's dark clarion

i scream the words of living

to save love's creatures from interminable tears
that i have known
since unbelievable absence became morning thief
of joyful abandon embodied in playful hugs
and lips' gentle passions

in this moment
i taste a lost dream of beauty
and its fleeting ephemera makes it all the more
          real
as i close my eyes
and accept the impermanence of the petals
that for hours have landed on my hair

unnoticed until this second's awakening to their
          presence
but flitting through my subconscious
so their history is no mystery to me
and i know they have reached out to me
all along

i sit as always i have yet in this now

i stop making decisions
to walk life's footpaths in linear programs
but in unforeseen embraces
unsensed until they arrive
not always in beauty

but nature's harmony smells of states of flowers
and reminds me that incense's temporary
       stimulation
draws its power not within the flame
but the memory of past burnings

i have clung to those flickering imaginations
in the candlelit recesses of mind
that never truly existed
while i lost the feeling of arms
pressing me into the togetherness of mutual
       understanding
and knowledge of tomorrows' promises kept

i return to the sound of water
not rushing

yet always
present
at the edge of my vision
as i open my eyes
to drink in the air of wind
i had not until i saw it
noticed brushing
the ends of my hair

not quite reaching to my eyes
but dancing beyond sight
as it strains at my scalp
ever gently
but consistently making me aware
that stillness is nothing more
than illusion

i stand and leave this place
by footsteps into the sun
still far from that twilight embrace of freedom to
          be myself
as is only possible now

as i know in days to come i will return

but new places to sit
will have replaced the old
as days' cycles turn
to whole lifetimes
in their minuscule changes
writ large on the canvas of the mountain
in varied colors
and passionate winds

in their endless impermanence
i once
only hours ago
found evidence of nature's deceit
and heard head's voices
demand human sacrifice
of all but my soul

yet its momentary existence saves me
as the words spoken once to me
amid sheets and dreams

shared with one now impossible to touch
in anything but spirit

being in that moment never lost to time's progress
but captured as canvased oil
beyond the skill of brushed masters
as its laughter becomes an archetype for my
        choice

to act not from a place of loss
but one of building new shimmering laughters
and hearing in them
what once was certain
living again in a self
i believed lost
but simply hidden

losing

the tears hiding behind my eyes reach out
to fall before your feet turn away but
they cling to the secrecy that's kept them from
      you all this time
i speak words without the passion that others feel
a desire to hold without the need to possess

i feel the distance that grows in the absence of
      nights of unclothed dancing
yet the intensity of this moment reflected in your
      gaze
impresses itself on my soul in ways bodies'
      rhythmic encounters sadly fall short of
      replicating
the instant my fingers touch your hair to brush it
      from your face amid shivering winds
i feel connected as hidden selves are pale
      imitations of

my hand in yours is a welcoming into a family of
        hope
not for minutes but lifetimes together
without the tension of games best left unplayed
or words said with no undo

where others shatter their togetherness for
            nighttimes of moistened pleasure
i walk in dreams in your footsteps following the
            same path
diverging but straying only the length of a word
before we face each other with smiles or tears

a single twitch of face
conveying more than all language hopes to match
notes played between your ears and mine
echo into distances unmapped
across fields of stars stretching into unseen
        futures now safe in the certainty of unlost
        partnership

the tears freed from their eye-bound prison fall
        onto footsteps once yours
now impressions in sand gently liquified with the
        salt from within me
i feel the sensation of your touch lingering on the
        cheek you brushed as you spoke of
        tomorrow hours away
but clouded vision through internal rain merely
        triggers an understanding of the need for
        sleep
before i drink your words and season them with
        the grasses through which we just walked

where you meet the horizon and the prisms before
        me turn body to dust
goodbye reverberates as if for the first time
as i dismiss the fear of betrayed speech
yet this moment is shaken by a knowledge of
        foreseen self-imposed tragedy

there is nothing within me to dispel the
        knowledge of uncertain afterlives

while i spoke in that few seconds amid
        conversation
of the absent theories
how i fear no death and in endless rebirths see no
        break
where you smiled in understanding yet it was you
        who was my teacher
without me taking it in until the lesson drowns
        me in my passive watching

i feel i am running as i chase you but in the first
        few steps i only walk yet stumble
picking up pace to find my feet following in
        seemingly limitless footsteps
reaching eons into a lapsed future the place where
        you disappeared at walking pace
hearing silence wakes me to the realization that i
        understood moments too late
the meaning of that first goodbye

yet sobbing at no distance melds with the
        overwhelming birdsong

no longer calming

triggering fears of a return to nature in climbing

        onto the wheel

to spin anew and land in unseen life of forgotten

        dreams

but movement beyond the edge of sight glints in

        sun's last rays and i turn

i hoped you would come you say before i catch my

        breath

in this moment i am free with you

hold me in the love we have only shared in

        thought

feel in me the passion of loss before it disappears

        into night

it sounds trite in my head as if it were prewritten

and i know it has echoed in your mind a thousand

        times as you walked away from me

unknowing if i would follow

to speak that confession into the lengthening
        shadows of the trees whose arms fail to
capture our souls

are you safe i speak in my head yet hear it against
        the backdrop of the branches
yet in reply you stare with eyes whose tears are
        less secretive than mine
but perhaps only so bold in this moment to make
        themselves known
your second attempt at goodbye comes with less
        spoken reality
more felt than sounded in my head

the eyes soaked in that instant close as
        understanding once again dawns too late
truth's loss in its unsounded words shatters
        birdsong as i scream a single piercing wail
yet i feel in your induced sleep a weak pulse and
        run the darkened paths with direction
        and purpose
i imagined impossible

tears streaming i am unwelcome in civilized
        company yet standing in the road that
        single car saw me
in time to stop without impact
a death i nearly dreamed of only for that second
if i were to fail you now not in hour of need but
        minute
we rediscovered you unmoved yet with barely
        sensed beating remaining within

the hours that follow tear me from myself as i sit
        atop the roof while you are saved below
        me
seeking punishment or salvation
i know only desire for them but without the
        pickiness to differentiate
neither comes from the heaven i scream at yet i
        cannot stop myself
gods not in my image but yours stream before my
        eyes as i hallucinate them into being

the moment you open your eyes in shock at
                having failed yourself
you smile
my tears no longer feel the need for secrecy as i
                hold your shivering hand in mine
thank you for saving me from myself
i speak the words to you

yet it feels as you have uttered the same
how you could not have known the unuttered
                goodbye was to have been mine
before in your pain i found myself whole in the
                touch of your fingers
somehow you feel the truth of what has happened

your eyes flicker with rebirth's joy
even in life's unexpected continuity
tomorrow has already arrived
my tears fall on our intertwined fingers as you
                drift back toward dreams

amused

i raise my head
from tear-filled hands
and lift eyes
to your secret face

as you speak
between my lips
unheard mysteries
amid lines of sorrow

to awaken distant ears
closed to all but lies
seeking metamorphosis
against sirened cliffs
of beckoned awakenings
where my soul seeks ends of fearlessness
and fires of welcomed damnation

i speak languages long dead
in the cavern

of your memory
welled up
in the vibrations
whose echoes unceasingly reign
in the kingdom of your new promise

broken for me
with each passing mouthful
of bloodied hatred shattered
into my vision

yet you call me
from beyond the existence
i seek
to shed
to awake
to the morning skylarks' melodies

to taste the eden
between your moments' panicked nakedness
and parched desire

i carry terrified instants
on shoulders narrowed
by worlds you create in me
as i am crushed
between odysseys' unproven myths
and winters' impacts
of irradiated insanity

torched into being
as inverted phoenix feathers
become digital quills
beneath myriad fingertips

yet unceasing momentary joys
escape
your mouth
and revive
an unfinished spirit
within me

casting moorings toward premoistened depths
to free me for the search

within you
for unwritten futures
to create

i touch within myself
sparks unbelievable before your flame
ignited a new rage
behind my eyes

to echo imagined rainbows
toward a world
where lies become
new histories
of races unrun
and colors
inseparable
in their diffuse majestic skintones
hiding impurities
with their white ideals

yet
i seek

the unforced darkness
of ink's virtual cousins
kissed onto paper
ith plasmid approximations of beauty

to call daydreamed meanderings
toward memory
as prompt for tomorrows
not yet written

you breathe life
no longer new or unexpected
through a version of me
built from a language
you taught me to speak

as your tongue's unmothering knowledge
tastes sweetly of nighttime secrets
felt in oceans of lust

and words appear
between my eyes and yours

with each unwilling breath
taken at your behest

yet in their now spoken freedom
my trapped self
is revealed
as it meets its inner elephant
existence by existence

and disappears in its union
with your soul's afterthoughts
to create joys
unfelt
without your kiss

fallen

raindrops glaze the pattern before my eyes
as i stare at twilight's cityscape
finding its life
after the haze of day
clears into the downpour of evening

traffic blends toward patterns
of bent reds and sweeping curves of white
as dancing dragons confiscate
the vehicles of human movement

buddha's bicycle has given itself
over to compassionless hogs
ridden by petrol-scented amazons
amid sexualized leather
and prismed chromium accents
unheard in an air of artificial thunder

were eyes closed
they could encounter the opposite

of senselessness
while clouds of heat amass
beneath the falling rain
to be dispersed in passing
and horns echo on moistened sidewalks
and feet trample the reverberations
through busyness' self-loathing
and mutually-unexpressed disinterest

war cries of the slightly inconvenienced
mingle with the wilderness of children
flowing the less-than-middle road
between play
and panic
and excitement
and fear
but indistinguishable in its sheer volume

undaunted by my lack of useless umbrella
careful feet carry me
from doorway to dripping arch
in search of a sense of you

but escape always came easily
to your shimmering eyes

a spirit floating on breeze
whose body one moment touched
with sensation unreal in its intensity
the next carried itself
no more solidly than ashes
scattered by the merest of breath
to climb mountains
unscalable by human endeavors

colors shattered
by the memory of moisture
hovering just beyond my vision
present themselves
as vision of togetherness
for a future i believe cannot happen
but i pretend comes every day
breathing another moment of existence

i step from solid ground onto wet grass

to feel the nature that has been stolen
from my waking hours
and find myself lost
in dreams of falling
between flowers
rich with the scent of openness
after lightning cleared the air

awake
to the reality of the moment
i see the ground
rushing
to catch my face
and realize hands have no chance
to prevent the instant sleep that awaits me
and i embrace it
as i kiss crushed petals
beneath my leaden form

i taste the aftereffects of contact
mingling with the bitterness of dandelion
on my lips

and sing praises
in whispers
for the nap among nature
in this momentary distraction
from the pretense of civilization

i leave part of myself
in that grass
as i stand
but refuse to brush its residue
from my imperfect shape
and welcome the next kiss
of kojin's fallen loves

flight

walking softened paths
into the shivering warmth
of the dawn forest
i resist momentary temptations
to lift my head to the sky
and scream to clouds
the question of rage behind my eyes
and force myself to continue
without direction
toward the semidarkness
of hate's beckoning sweetness

your memory lingers
on a skin scorched
by the cleansing waters of self-immolation
yet all of my desperate attempts
to wash you from the echoes of touch
that once within me
you made life find itself
fail completely

and you rise from charred singed self
to resonate
unconfined by body or time

i walk as were i marching
willingly to battle's dishonored death
yet no enemy awaits me
within these trees' shadowed confines

your voice calls to me
not of passion but love that i recognize
as the temptation
away from the evil
that once inhabited my every thought
and was torn from my actions
by the goodness
i once pretended

i ask myself unanswered questions
of the reality of those lyrics
now spinning in the air
between leaves and branches

and tiny mammals no longer hiding
from my rhythmic progression

yet no insight appears
and you live there before me
slightly unseen
yet just this moment
disappeared
behind the trunk of another barrier
to holding the you of substance
whether substantial you may be
i know not
yet doubt not an instant

you catch my eyes
with the shimmering of your fingertips
caressing a single leaf
within my line of sight
and i turn my head
to connect with yours

eyes or fingers

i cannot tell which i reach out
to bring back to this life
yet either would suddenly mean your presence
shifts from after to before
and my questing path
would not so much have found its end
but lost its beginning's impetus

yet nothing beyond droplets
quivering in rivulets atop miniature streams
appears within the folds of the leaf
on which my eyes fall
the moment before the moisture from within
again seeks escape
through eyes
onto a face newly aged
with an echo
of those creases the leaf embodies
more naturally

forward is the end i accept
yet cannot speak the word of

into silence
or behind the veil of forest noise
in fear that in its utterance
it disappears
and i will be dragged
by those of my own species i abhor
who could chain me to the present
and tear future's absence
from my fingers
before ever it appears
from dream into reality

a dream in which i play
no role but observer
and hand to you the power to decide
a future that i know
you would not select for me
but in my desperation
i see no other path
into the life that you once called me
to live
within your field of vision

and between hands that taught me
that love resides elsewhere
but in lust's performance

blue distracts a moment
as jay's wings suddenly connect
with the stream's surface
and i turn
toward a new direction
whose end lies not in place
but absence of time

alone
i watch solitary movement
in an air whose currents uphold
and move that body
far more fragile than mine
and in that lost direction i hear
the taste of your command to live
where you could not
and survive
faced with places

you left behind

yet i turn ears from your words
and walk nearing a run
in the focus
toward the higher points
mere steps from the place
where bird and eye connected
in the creation of a new memory

i see no you
hovering above the ledge in the distance
yet tears fragment not the certainty
that flows within me
that in the absence of ground beneath my feet
the moment of life's end
is entangled once again
being held by your eyes' unfailing warmth
and words' joy
in the instant act of life

the air once surrounding

only above and beside
fills dreams of flight
impossible only in their continuance
and possible only once
before inert inaction
returns to the forest
and i give myself to the future
not of soaring but the sinking of self
as stone in the river below
these tens of meters
into which my weighted self
may only fall once
never to regain the surface

i feel the air whispering
in tones only calling me to an afterlife
i know is myth
but in the end of sadness
a hope exists for me

in this moment
there is no sound of forest and wind

but the memory of your laughter
that i have not shared

and i cannot jump
and combine the tears
at my ending
with yours

life's beauty died with you
yet in each second
i live
those memories
into the next

unwilling to lose you with my own end
yet the love i hold within me
is bounded by the tears
i cannot for a moment shed
and a life
tortured by a smile i no longer possess
within myself
as the lessons of you were lost

when death embraced you

as once you held me

coding

in this moment

if you change your heart

it reprograms your mind

and through running that program

it creates a new life

yet as with all simple things

i locked my heart in a cage

and built it a rigid skeleton

so it couldn't move

or breathe

or shift

or change

and in its rigidity

it wrote not a single line of code

for my mind

living tradition my mind

became more afraid

with each passing moment

and learned to do nothing

but wallow in its fear

they tell me
there is nothing to fear
but itself
and they are not wrong
but fear is plenty
to cause limitless terror
in each instant i live
when that fear has endless potential
to come true
and the world around me
is not simply the cause of boundless nightmares
but the source of reminders
from all too prevalent
and willing
and anxious
and joyful others
pretending to be friends
telling me stories of themselves and others
living the panic
i find within myself

and they smile

at the discomfort they live into the world

and the mindbending clarity

they wish into me

with each passing word

but they continue to act as friends

as if subverting my every day's attempt

to continue

to recover

to believe

to breathe

to focus

to do anything with my life

other than shiver in fear

is their purpose and desire

and that it is somehow normal

to hurt those you say you love

with images of disgust

and ideas of pain

that stay with them

through nights of shivering

and mornings of sweat-coated tears

i pretend to let my heart live
outside its box
but the cage remains

i may learn the secret to freedom
for the voices that reside in my soul
but now they scream endless curses
and repeated reminders
that i am living
the nightmare of my own creation
echoed in the vision
of those around me

a future may save me
but i don't believe

aflame

why do nightingales cry

in the predawn calm

is it pain or relief

or simply disgust at the future

that they know is coming

to haunt our days

while they watch

in the cinema of trees

i can predict

none of their intentions

in screaming their lament

tones wild

with the imagination of we witnesses

to the crimes of our siblings

yet we as they

helpless to change the path

on which we are walking

more than our feet can reach

in any moment

although i would

if i could reach my hands up

and escape this place

leave the globe

on which i am

helplessly spinning

and leap into a place

any place

distant from here

to take my chances

and gamble on a future

not built on blocks

of certain misery

they speak to me

with their wings of possibilities

as they are not

confined

to this place
and to this time
as are we earthbound mortals
whose feet carry us
not to distant realms
but simply to the horrors
before our faces

i too wish i could sing
that morning song
of lament
and watch in anxious anticipation
some new day
of self-destructive prowess
of humanity casting itself
into the fires
of our own making
with nothing of the horror
i now feel
but simply to watch
as were it on a screen
of artifice's malignant instruction

a story
of my own making
in my mind
for entertainment only

but truth becomes
not stranger than the lies
but founded in a hatred
i could never have imagined possible

and still i find myself fighting
against my hopes
with each passing sunset
to believe this path is true

as tribes reform
with heads shaven
and colors
separated
in skin and flag
and language and prayer

directions indicating protection
and humanity
and creating an other
without the spark of life's divine beauty
or even the potential for it to arrive
except in belonging

to give up the self
to recreate it
in the image of a god
of war and possession
and to disavow
the unity
that holds us
not simply as a race
but as a species
on survivals' brinks
too numerous to name

the edge of a cliff
not crumbling but as vapor

on the fast-approaching winter winds

a frost that is all-consuming
and which the nightingales warn us of
in their throaty clarion

that we are but mortals
no better and no different
no higher on chains
or spinning orbs
climbing into no heaven
but that of our own making

and sinking into a fiery state
as forests turn
to smoke and flame and ash
and we follow their example
as we give paper and plastic
with signs of bisected curves
to the demons
of segregation
and call back a new era

of nationhood

subjecting all
to our traditional hatreds
yet tomorrow
they will sing
and each tomorrow

as we fight
to create days
for ourselves
where others may not inhabit

and die
while in those predawn moments
the song outlives us
in its shimmering

About the Author

Avi is a teacher and writer, one who desires to live outside the boundaries of a society lost to the artifice of equality trampled by misogyny, racism, and sexualized oppression, one who lives apart from the constructions of gender identity while crying for the necessity of that existence being apart from a world in fragments because of its unwillingness to shed its traditional attachment to manufactured roles.

They have lived and studied between Canada's east and west coasts, composing poetry on the shores of the Atlantic and pacific, holding dear within the heart the solitude that comes from standing at the edge of land with feet no longer willing to turn back toward humanity's lost humanity.

They are a proponent of art as an unrelenting
walk along the pathway of beauty where ideas and
thoughts and reality and existence take secondary
role to language as a conduit for the simple
pleasure of words living for their capacity to take
the listener, the reader, even the writer to new
worlds deep not in their knowledge but in their
pure escape into beauty itself.

in thought truth may arrive
or perhaps it remains absent
yet without a desire to know
lies shall be your only sanctuary